The Tao
of Recovery

Jim McGregor

THE
TAO OF
RECOVERY

A Quiet Path to Wholeness

BANTAM BOOKS
New York   Toronto   London   Sydney   Auckland

THE TAO OF RECOVERY
A Bantam Book / February 1992

Library of Congress Cataloging-in-Publication Data
McGregor, Jim.
   The Tao of recovery : a quiet path to wholeness / by Jim
McGregor.
      p. cm.
   ISBN 0-553-08029-6
   1. Lao-tzu. Tao te ching. 2. Compulsive behavior—Religious
aspects. I. Title. II. Title: Recovery.
BL1900.L36M32   1992
299'.514448—dc20   91–22924
                                                              CIP

Published simultaneously in the United States and Canada

Bantam Books are published by Bantam Books, a division of Bantam Doubleday Dell
Publishing Group, Inc. Its trademark, consisting of the words "Bantam Books" and the
portrayal of a rooster, is Registered in U.S. Patent and Trademark Office and in other
countries. Marca Registrada. Bantam Books, 666 Fifth Avenue, New York, New York
10103.

PRINTED IN THE UNITED STATES OF AMERICA

BVG   0 9 8 7 6 5 4 3 2 1

Contents

Preface   *ix*

PART I: BEING   *1*

The Mystery of Recovery   *3*
Flowing with the River   *5*
Knowing Myself   *7*
Trying Too Hard   *9*
Allow   *11*
Strange Thinking   *13*
Waiting   *15*
Easy Does It   *17*
The Mountaintop Is Rocky   *19*
I Surrender to Humility   *21*
Another Paradox   *23*
I Am Here   *25*
I Can't Explain It   *27*
"If I Can Explain It, That's Not It"   *29*
I Now Understand   *31*
Returning   *33*

PART II: AWAKENING   *35*

Awareness   *37*
Wishing Will Not Make It So   *39*
Where Are My Feelings?   *41*

Insecure 43

Up and Down 45

Complacency 47

My Desires Hold Me Back 49

Stopping Short 51

No Mind 53

Nothing Is Forever 55

Quiet 57

Emptiness Is Fullness 59

Sickness 61

There Is More 63

I Am Different 65

I Am Childlike 67

Names 69

The Universe Is Small 71

PART III: RECOVERING 73

Powerless Is Powerful 75

Competition 77

Power in the Present 79

Contentment 81

Robber Barons 83

Lose and Win 85

Endings 87

I Won But I Lost 89

Gain and Loss 91

Success Is Not Success 93

Less Is More 95

The System 97

Unfair 99

Life Overvalued   101
Withered and Dry   103
Helping But Hurting   105
Work Without Working   107
Force   109
Nonviolence   111
I See Without Looking   113

PART IV: LIVING   115

Community   117
Nature   119
Obligations   121
A Small Risk   123
Detachment   125
I Am Restless   127
Moderation   129
Low Lands   131
Motives   133
Heroes   135
Leaders Are Not Leaders   137
Chaos Attracts "Experts"   139
Cleverness   141
Cunning and Baffling   143
Meddling   145
Minding My Own Business   147
Nonaction Is Not No-action   149
Where Are All the Others?   151
Judge Not—Fear Not   153
Virtue   155
What is Great?   157

Small and Simple Are Great   159
Living But Dead   161
Responsibility   163
Abandonment   165
Hope   167
Abundance   169

Preface

The words and thoughts expressed in this book have come to me after many years of close attachment to the *Tao Te Ching* and my personal experiences with the recovery process.

Lao Tzu, a wise man who lived nearly twenty-six centuries ago in China, is credited with creating the eighty-one verses that make up the beautiful book, *Tao* (the way or path) *Te* (virtue) *Ching* (sacred book). The *Tao* has been translated more often than any other book except for the Bible.

The Tao suggests a universal order that is ever present, reliable, and mystical in that it is beyond explanation. It calls for acceptance beyond understanding.

The Tao of Recovery is a series of interpretive passages written in response to the *Tao Te Ching*. Each passage deals with an issue of recovery.

In recent years, the word *recovery* has come to be associated with drug and alcohol rehabilitation. A more liberal interpretation would include a wide spectrum of dysfunctional ways of being, including co-dependency, which is a relationship negatively affected by the addiction of someone else.

For every addicted person, there are a number of others who also have been negatively affected, including family, friends, and business associates. Those of us who are in that position must learn to reclaim our self-esteem and take our rightful, healthy place in society. We must do this whether or not the addicted person is able to do this too. (Most of my writing centers on issues of co-dependency because these have been my experiences.)

I consider the *Tao Te Ching*, or the *Book of The Way* as it is also known, an excellent companion in our recovery. For those of us who have a problem with the God concept in twelve-step programs, the Tao offers a safe haven. It makes no demands. The ideas of detachment, letting go, acceptance, and the recognition of some presence that I can rely upon to transcend my human fallibility are all inherent in the Tao.

The Tao represents one of the essentials of recovery from any malady: the discovery within oneself of serenity, of calm, of peace. Whether one's problem is simple unhappiness or the feelings of unfulfillment that are a part of so many of our lives, whether depression or illness or living with physical disabilities— in all of these situations you can find yourself responding to the gifts of the Tao. My own gifts have included acceptance, serenity, and renewed self-esteem.

Ideally, our recovery efforts are directed toward achieving an inner spiritual unity as well as a oneness in relation to our universe and fellow human beings.

The *Tao Te Ching* and my own twelve-step program have provided me with a foundation that has given me the freedom to find peace and serenity in my own way. Although I came to understand that my nature has a strong pull toward the softer, less aggressive way, some of my friends who see things in a more linear way have also found that the Tao has gradually worked its way into their lives.

Repetition of ideas and concepts is an essential part of the Tao and twelve-step programs, and you will notice the same tendency in *The Tao of Recovery*. Repetition is helpful in grasping the deeper meanings, the profound and simple essence of the Tao and of the twelve steps. Even though we may have heard something over and over again, sometimes suddenly we will understand it as if we had really just heard it for the first time. Avoid trying to "figure it out." Just read it and let it go. You will be amazed at how often the deeper meaning will manifest itself. When I reread passages from the *Tao Te Ching*, the message is often completely different from former readings of the same material. The supply is inexhaustable.

Lao Tzu's writings on the Tao are often presented with the humor of the ancient sages. In view of this, I have also had fun with some of the chapter titles.

I have used the word *Tao* sparingly in this work because I would like each person who reads this to choose freely the word that best describes their own "higher power" or "God."

You will note the use of *Great Mother* in my book. Great Mother simply reflects the effect that the Tao has had on me over the years. The many messages of acceptance and inner reflection strike me as feminine qualities, and it is not hard for me to envision the process of recovering using the Tao as similar to a mother or grandmother watching over her children.

This leads me to my most heartfelt message. I am not attempting to teach you anything, nor to present a self-help program. My hope is that I can share something of value with you by relating those thoughts that came to me upon reading a particular verse of the *Tao Te Ching*.

I give you my humble effort with no expectations. Please read it when you want to and in whatever order you wish.

The Tao
of Recovery

PART I

BEING

The Mystery of Recovery

The mystery of recovery cannot be explained!

The path is dim and thinly veiled, and at times there is total darkness. Like all things that are truly precious, recovery presents itself on its own schedule and in its own way.

The path is formless; it cannot be grasped.

The path is silent; it cannot be heard.

The path is nothing; it cannot be seen.

I will learn about the worldly aspects of recovery and then let myself go onto the path of the unknown, for this is where I will find my peace and serenity.

Flowing with the River

The universal order of things leaves nothing out. If I am in tune with the God of my understanding, like water, my serenity flows everywhere.

Those situations and relationships to which there seemed no hope are no longer hopeless.

I will use a gentle approach that comes from quietness and truth. When I am ready, the answers that are for my highest and best will arrive as though they floated down the river to me.

I will be found floating down the river of the unknown, and I let go of the upstream struggle forever.

- a willow which bends
- you cannot harm me unless I let you

Knowing Myself

I will never really know myself until I find my place in the natural order.

Since I prefer the simple and easy way, I can begin, right now, to accept that I do have a place in the universe.

Then I can start my self-examination by recognizing my strengths first and my areas of opportunity for growth next.

It is not easy and I may not be ready now, but I am willing to start when the time is right.

I will know when that time arrives.

Step Four

Trying Too Hard

As long as I keep "trying" to recover, I deprive myself of the beauty of true recovery, which is spiritual in nature and is presented as a gift.

I can see some results from my willful efforts. These manifestations of my own efforts served me well in my early recovery, but it is time to move on.

There is much beyond my understanding.

I will be open to these mysteries of recovery that will arrive when I become open to total acceptance and love.

· keep it by giving it away

Allow

My youth was dominated by severe restrictions placed upon me by unreasonable parents. I became cunning and deceitful and learned to hate myself.

My close friend had the opposite experience. Her parents didn't care enough to give her any guidelines. We are both products of dysfunctional homes and don't see any hope for ourselves.

But there is hope.

I will begin an honest inner searching for the strength of the universe.

I will listen to those who have found the way.

My life will change if I will allow it to.

- listen to the oldtimers — but they were newcomers once
- the oldtimers are not necessarily in the program (eg. Ren D.)

Strange Thinking

I have the courage to allow myself to be behind and to wait for
whatever it is that is supposed to come my way.

Simplicity is the way of the wise.

Humility is the way of the great.

Bending is the way of long life.

Yielding is the way of the strong.

I just have to let spirit fill me with the knowing that the
mystical, and nonrational answers will arrive.

I am waiting!

Dr Bob said: "let's not loose this
cup — keep it simple"
First things First

Waiting

Challenges can become larger than life.

My immediate reaction to challenges is to attack and conquer. This has not worked in the past.

Withdrawing and waiting for the "enemy" to make his move gives one time to understand the enemy's strengths and weaknesses.

Thus it gives one a tremendous advantage.

When I apply this approach to my challenges, I find that they often disappear and never again arise.

My calm and confident attitude allows me to move through these challenges easily and without distress.

This is called overcoming challenges without trying.

· pray for your enemy

Easy Does It

Since there are opposites to all things, I will choose the easy instead of the difficult way.

I can choose relaxation or stress, detachment or control, acceptance or dominance, freedom or attachment, peace or strife, joy or sorrow, and bliss or misery.

I will remember that when the hard way presents itself, it is only one side of things and doesn't deserve my attention.

When my mind is at rest and I am empty and receptive, the easy and beautiful unfolding takes place. This is known as recovering the easy way.

- I can chose
- opening the "channel"
- Step Eleven

The Mountaintop Is Rocky

I live in the valley, where all things flow down to me. Neither struggle nor effort is needed.

Reaching the mountaintop is more difficult.

Right now I am recovering, and "reaching mountaintops" is not one of my priorities.

Acceptance and allowing things to happen for me is in contrast to that which I have been taught.

I will consider where the ambition and acquisitiveness of that past have led me.

I now choose the softer, more accepting way of life that has led others to peace and harmony.

• Easy does it

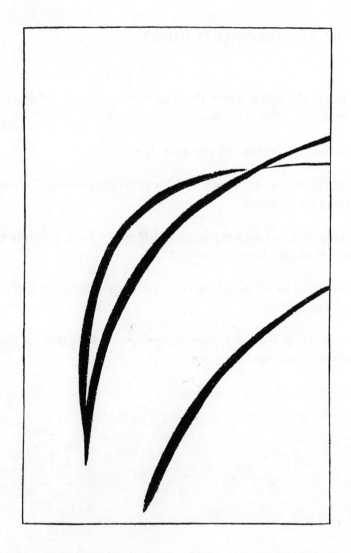

I Surrender to Humility

Humility is the quiet acceptance of my place in the natural order of things. Both arrogance and low self-esteem are gone when I am humble.

Surrender is associated with shame in the secular world. Does this mean that I should constantly be at war with the world in order to be "somebody"?

Well, I am "somebody," and I got here by surrendering to the universal order, which might be called God or Spirit or Tao. It doesn't matter how or why I surrendered because that was the beginning of true humility in my life.

Now that I have no need to be other than I am, I am open to all of the gifts of recovery and will surely become other than I am, to the benefit of all: myself, my family, my friends, and the universe.

- humility is real
- white is the international symbol for surrender

Another Paradox

Soft and yielding overcomes the strong and stiff.

Solid as a rock—what a hoax!

I was that person that everyone counted on, and I fell apart.
Devastation is the product of this scenario, both for the "rock"
and for those who are leaning on him.

There is no rock that has not, is not, or will not be covered by
water, that soft, pliable substance that you can touch but not
feel.

There is no human (rock) that has not, is not, or will not be
covered by the spirit of the unknown. This includes both life and
death.

There is no place for me to hide by showing myself to be great.

There is a wonderful place for me in the stream of life as a
humble, soft, and pliable being who paradoxically overcomes all.

∘ you keep it by giving it away

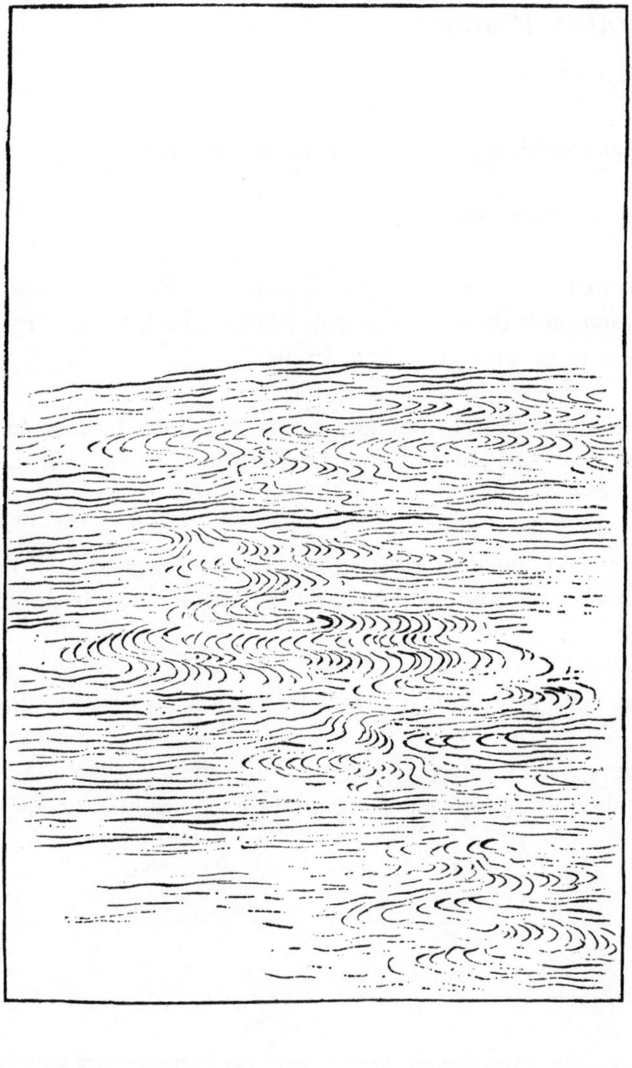

I Am Here

I am in the natural flow of the universe!

It is the one thing that is eternal, and I can count on it, even though it is always in motion, flowing far away but always returning. I will not resist since this is man's natural place in the universal order.

Many of us were not aware of the natural flow of all around us until we became aware of our obsessions and dependencies and sought help. Many more of us have still not become aware. I grieve for them.

Resting in the Mother of the universe is exactly what I need in order to participate in the world around me.

I am thankful for arriving here, however painful the trip.

· gratitude

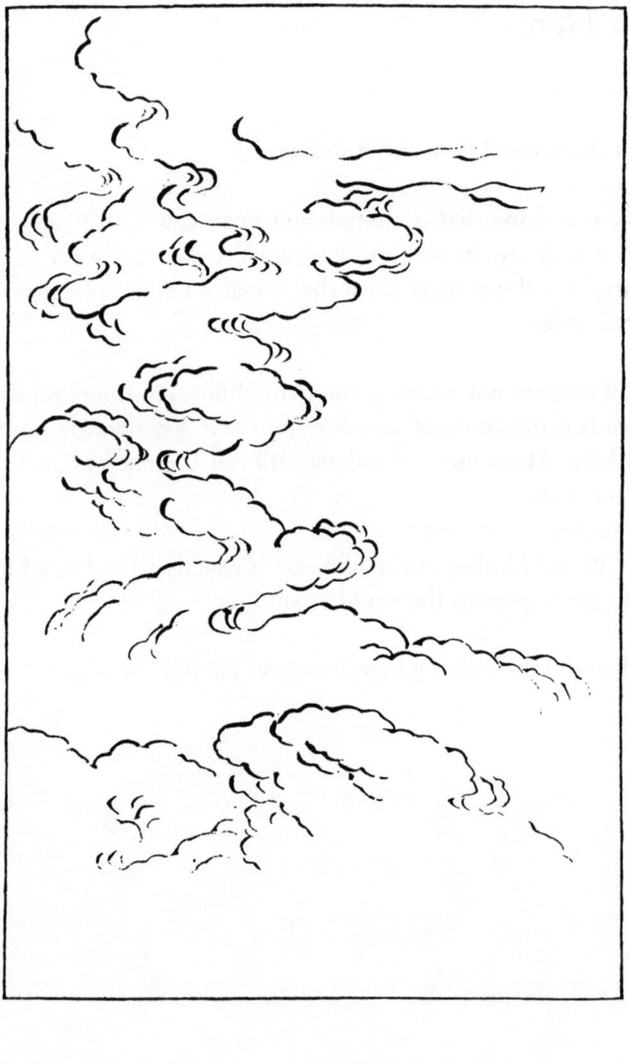

I Can't Explain It

I am filled with the wonderful feeling of "knowing" the source of all things without having to know how it all happened.

At times, I have been sure that there was no supreme being, and at times I was disappointed after I learned what I was supposed to do and expect regarding conventional religion.

The universal order is elusive and intangible; dim and dark but not without substance.

Since the beginning of consciousness, mankind has been aware of a presence "beyond" and has demonstrated that awareness in widely divergent ways.

Therefore my peace and serenity require no explanation.

- trust a Higher Power

"If I Can Explain It, That's Not It"

The universe, in the spiritual sense, is a limitless void that is ever present and is never filled. I cannot understand it, nor explain it.

My place in the natural order is important yet need not be known. I am nothing, but I am everything. My life can be wonderful even though no one else understands or knows who I am.

Resting in the knowing that I don't have to struggle to find my rightful place in the universe allows me to be easy, peaceful, and serene.

If you eat Bran, you won't have to.

I Now Understand

Yield and overcome.
Bend and be straight.
Empty and be full.
Wear out and be new.
Have little and gain.
Have much and be confused.

This is my favorite verse from the *Tao Te Ching*. But it was totally backward when I first read it. However, accepting the unexplainable is one of the gifts of my spiritual recovery.

My first efforts at letting go were self-willed, but the best I could do. Time and the support of some enlightened friends have helped me to comprehend the wisdom of this message.

I was lucky! I was forced to surrender, forced to make amends, lost everything, and now have everything that I value—peace, serenity, and loving relationships.

I now understand.

Let go.

Returning

Like the tides, the clouds, the sun, and the flow of the universe itself, I move away and back again.

Sometimes it is frightening to lose my sense of well-being. Always it is unpleasant.

In the natural order there are excesses and scarcities such as floods and droughts, violent storms and doldrums. But things return to normal.

Why would I expect to be above the natural order?

The awareness that I am a part of the natural order is an indescribable gift.

I am grateful.

• Dame Fortune's Wheel

PART II

AWAKENING

Awareness

Awareness is an important part of the recovery process. It is the beginning of self-discovery.

We all want to become that beautiful, loving person. The awareness that this is possible is an integral part of the conscious recovery process.

Awareness relieves me of the necessity of deciding whether I am good or not.

Awareness will allow me to be good without knowing it.

Wishing Will Not Make It So

Wishing that I were someone else—more famous, wealthier, stronger, more beautiful, or more serene—is destructive to my well-being.

By changing my attitude of wishing and fantasizing to that of acceptance and gratitude, I will no longer be devastated by disappointments and losses.

Being famous, wealthy, strong, beautiful, or serene is fine but not required for my well-being.

The reality of the present moment is my starting point. I can choose to let go and allow the growth process to begin, or I can continue to fantasize and stay where I am.

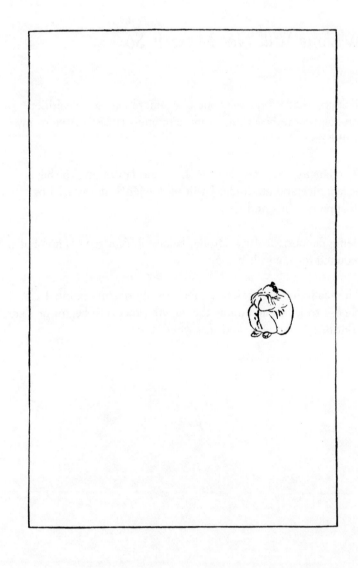

Where Are My Feelings?

My eyes can be my enemy!

There is so much illusion in the world today, it is impossible to determine that which is real and that which is really illusion.

Much of my life has been spent in running after sights, sounds, and tastes with the notion that I may miss out on something. Most of my running has been dictated by my eyes.

The tremendous impact of advertising and the fantasies that it creates has practically obliterated my ability to feel.

The real beginning of my recovery will come when I begin to listen to my feelings, both joyful and painful, knowing that these are real and can be trusted.

Insecure

I am brash.
I am cynical.
I am critical.
I am aggressive.

I am insecure!

The universal order is quiet.
The universal order is accepting.
The universal order is never-ending.

The universal order is humble and full!

I will join the universal order when I am ready.

I will then be humble and full.

Up and Down

Since the true nature of things is cyclical, sometimes I am up and sometimes I am down. These cycles can be violent when I am out of sync with the universe, or mild when I am in tune.

I remember the intense fear when I was at my bottom. I wish that I had understood that there was no place to go but up. However, at that point I was not capable of rational thought.

Knowing that everything is always in motion and moves in cycles comforts me.

My cycles are now natural and comfortable. I don't particularly like the lows, but I now understand that they are simply the other side of the highs.

Complacency

Am I complacent and lazy, or do I just appear that way?

Resting in the secular world restores the physical body but not the deep inner yearning.

Continual resting in the secular world might well be complacent and lazy.

Resting in the Great Mother appears complacent, but is the natural way.

By listening to my inner voice, I will know when it is time to move on.

Like all answers, when I am in tune with the universal order, the answer is simple and easy. . . .

It really doesn't matter!

My Desires Hold Me Back

My intense desire for change often thwarts any effort I make to achieve that which I desire.

I admire those who exhibit a strong sense of the present moment and are alert to those things that are going on around them. But they seem not to be caught up in the attending excitement. They seem remote.

The remoteness and composure that these individuals exhibit allow them to wait for the right time before taking any action.

Often the action they choose yields to the existing conditions and avoids unnecessary conflict.

By not seeking fulfillment, I can rest in the knowledge that my life will not be dominated by the unhealthy obsession to change.

Stopping Short

Enough is enough!

There is never enough. Stopping is never an option. Stretching the limits sounds heroic but usually leads to tragedy.

Recovery is dependent upon stopping short:

Stopping short of obsessive actions of the past.

Stopping short of frantic action to correct those actions of the past.

Stopping short of the obsession to gain instant serenity.

Wealth and material possessions can be taken away.

Mental gymnastics to gain power, possessions, and prestige leave one vulnerable to destruction.

I will remember that enough is enough.

No Mind

By having a mind of my own, I knew who was right and who was wrong. I knew who was good and who was bad.

I did not love those whom I considered bad. In some cases I hated them.

Was that wrong? How would I know, since I now don't know right from wrong anymore?

What made me change so much?

First was the realization that I had completely reversed my beliefs of the past. Second, those things that I just had to have proved unfulfilling.

That is not much of a reward for having a mind of my own.

I now choose No Mind, that egoless attitude of acceptance, and the attendant peace and serenity.

Nothing Is Forever

Nothing is forever, but No Thing is eternal.

What do I mean by that?

All things of the human world can be taken away, by death, if not before. The No Thing, the unexplainable universal order, is, has been, and always will be there.

Things of the human world—material possessions, wealth, friendships, and family—are wonderful if I can avoid obsessing over them and being destroyed when they are taken away.

Happiness, joy, and contentment are human qualities that when allowed to take their own course can lead to more.

The universal order, under whatever name I choose, is ever present and eternal and always available.

Quiet

I rest in the Great Mother of the universe. When I am truly at rest, I can live fully in the secular world and avoid the distractions of greed, violence, and false love.

When I am quiet and talk little, I hear much.

When I am not quiet and talk much, I hear nothing.

When I am quiet and guard the senses, I feel much.

When I am not quiet and I am busy, I feel little.

When I am quiet and centered, life is full.

When I am not quiet and centered, life is beyond hope.

Yielding, bending, and going inside with an open heart are the ways of the Great Mother.

Emptiness Is Fullness

Emptiness makes us nervous!

Yet it is the empty spaces that make everything possible to exist. Can you imagine a universe with no empty spaces?

So why does the thought of an empty mind sound so negative?

The rewards for an empty mind are boundless, as long as we are willing to allow it to fill when it is ready. I can choose immediately to replace the emptiness with new positive thoughts and gain temporary relief, or I can make another, more lasting choice.

I can choose the natural order of the universe to fill my empty mind when the time is ripe.

This solution comes from the great unknown and will be a permanent part of my life.

Sickness

I didn't know that I was sick. I didn't like it when you told me I was sick.

I am sick of sickness, and I am on the path to recovery.

My body is strong.

My mind is clear.

My spirit soars.

I am in the flow of the universe.

Thank you, Great Mother, for my sickness and the wisdom to accept it as such.

There Is More

That which is mysterious and invisible and always present is now a part of my life.

At one time I despised myself and feared and distrusted everyone. I could not be trusted, since I had not yet accepted that I was the problem.

Not long ago, I was resting comfortably in the knowledge that I was worthy of spiritual love, and I thought that contentment would result. But something told me that I could be more than simply content.

With a lot of support from a lot of loving people, my loving place in the universal order is now conceivable to me.

I have changed, and I am open to all the changes that are still to come.

I Am Different

I have always been different and didn't fit in. Or was it only that I thought I didn't? It doesn't matter now, for I know that I am different and I love it.

When I was traumatized by the terror of my life before recovery, I felt that my situation was unique.

When I began to recover, I found a whole new world full of those who understood and had been exactly where I had been.

A burden was lifted. Now I am different again.

I am alone among friends.

I am aimless but sure.

I am detached but aware.

I am in the present, only.

Enlightenment is completeness.

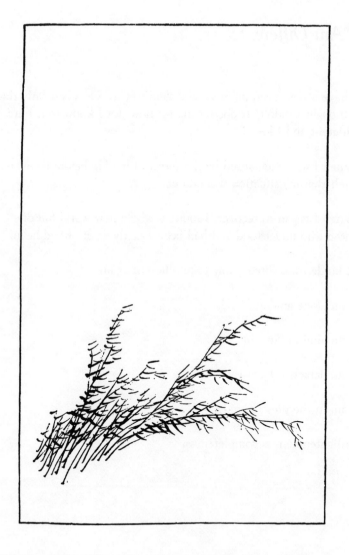

I Am Childlike

I am in the stream of life without distractions. Why should I concern myself with all the things of this world that are beyond my control?

Controversial issues outside my area of interest impede my recovery. I have found that yielding and bending work best when dealing with issues that concern me.

The simple pleasures of life are the bedrock upon which I stand, allowing those with unlimited ambition and zeal the questionable privilege of "running the world."

I am uncomplicated and detached. I therefore have the time and humility to care for others.

I am a child of the universe.

Names

Names...

Christian, Buddhist, Muslim...

German, American, Chinese, Polish...

Man, woman, child, boy, girl...

Names are useful but also define and separate us from each other.

We are all one....

We are all part of the universe....

If we only knew it!

The Universe Is Small

The universe is every-where, and it is no-where. It is small, and it is large. It is aimless, and it takes care of all things.

The natural order of things is neither good nor bad; it exists forever, and it doesn't exist.

The mystery of the universal order defies my understanding, but I know that it is there and that I have a place in it. It demands nothing and gives what I need.

The "whatever it is" is great in the sense of a truly great person. It is quiet and unobtrusive so that I hardly know that it is there, but it is there for us all.

PART III

RECOVERING

Powerless Is Powerful

Being in the natural flow, there is no need to be first. Being behind is where I need to be if I am going to be truly useful to my community and friends.

Being lower allows all good to flow down, and when that good is shared, all are protected.

There is no master and pupil, no stronger and weaker.

Powerless is powerful!

By serving humbly, one is supported.

By not competing, one does not meet competition.

Competition

Competing to conquer and hurt is destructive to others and to myself. Competing to survive is sometimes necessary. Competing for fun is healthy when losing is not a tragedy.

The prevalent concept of competition, "winning is everything," leads to corruption in government, business, sports, and even in our personal relationships. How could we accept such a concept?

I have won a number of "competitions," and it felt great. When I lost, it felt terrible.

I now know a better way. Compete and do my best to win as long as I am kind, true to myself and my God, and willing to accept the results. This is in the natural order of things.

The most destructive competition is with myself. . . . It is poison!

Power in the Present

Civilizations have always been ruthless. Man continues to struggle for the power of money, dominance, position, or fame as a substitute for true spiritual enlightenment.

It is rare for a person of power truly to respect those whom they view as less powerful. It is not rare for the people of power to lose their power because they have no center.

I do not need to prove myself by the acquisition of power in its corrupt form. I choose to join the truly powerful who are caring and serene among all people and all conditions.

My spiritual growth begins with the acceptance of where I am and continues with the acceptance of the natural order, for all things.

Contentment

I want money, houses, cars, furs, stereos, friends, and . . . contentment!

I have everything that I need, but I want more. Then I will be secure.

But will I be content?

My inner space is empty, and I have tried so hard to be fulfilled that I am tempted to give up.

It seems that I have treated spiritual fulfillment as I have treated cars, money, and houses. I want it and I am fighting for it.

I have heard that desires cause pain. I have heard that peace and serenity are already present in me, if I will only allow them to manifest.

I believe that I will give up the fight and wait for the beautiful gift of contentment.

Robber Barons

When I begin to envy those with wealth, fame, and splendor, do I remember the millions who are starving and whose lives have absolutely no meaning?

Our culture admires wealth, fame, and splendor, and I am a part of the culture.

I cannot change the culture, but I can live in it, walking the middle road and not straying onto the path of greed and insecurity.

At times I am depressed with humanity's direction.

This is not the way of the universal order.

Lose and Win

Some of us have lost everything—loved ones, possessions, money, businesses, and ourselves. What a tragedy!

Many of us can look back on these losses as the beginning of our recovery. It appears that this kind of a crisis is necessary for us to become willing to look honestly at ourselves and our place in the universe.

Loved ones, possessions, money, businesses, and even our identity have no permanence and can be lost at any time. No one, even the saints among us, can avoid this possibility.

What to do? Nothing!!!

Knowing that all is temporary except the universal order, I can relax in the knowledge that now that I am in harmony with the universe, losses will not be losses.

Endings

I have failed often in the past.

Failure arrived just as I was about to succeed. Why?

Am I afraid to succeed?

Am I not worthy of success?

Maybe I should start out with small, easy steps and let things work themselves out naturally. If my expectations are not too high, it might be easier to allow success to arrive.

I will give the same gentle attention to both the beginning and the end.

I Won But I Lost

There are so many wars going on in the world that it is hard to avoid them. The war against drugs, the wars of business dominance, the wars of sports, and the real wars of killing are ever present and disastrous.

I won my personal war of success and left behind a trail of destruction in the winning. The injured included loved ones, competitors, clients, our ethical culture, and our world. And myself!

If I rejoice in winning at all costs, I must love inflicting pain and suffering on my brothers and sisters.

Is that really me?

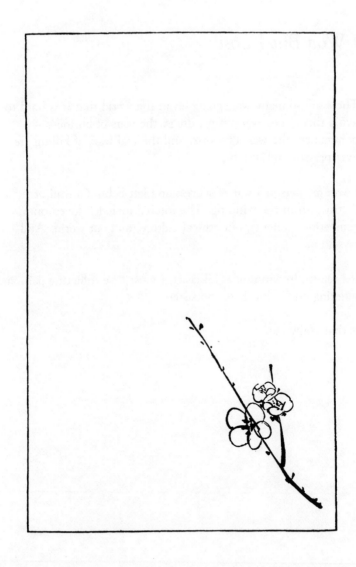

Gain and Loss

I had much, and I now have little. That is how it looks to the rest of the world.

I had little, and I now have much. That is how it looks to me.

Has recovery made me irrational? Probably, when viewed by the "normal" people. But I have a secret!

I now have me!

If I was wealthy before recovery, that is fine.

If I am still wealthy, that is fine.

If I have little now but I have me, I have everything I need and that is fine.

This is what I know. . . . I had to lose me before I could find me. Wealth and possessions were not a factor.

Success Is Not Success

Success and fame call for extraordinary effort and often lead one to an attitude of self-righteousness.

Even those of us whose lives don't include notoriety can take on the extra burden of self-righteousness.

Putting on a show takes away from our real selves.

Boasting subjects us to ridicule.

Bragging makes us look foolish.

Having too much success makes others resentful. The stress of guarding our possessions and our position leads us away from peace and serenity.

I am truly successful when I have found my rightful place in the universe and when I have served mankind without knowing how.

Less Is More

Until now, I have spent my life doing more and learning more. Can there be anything wrong with that? I am beginning to wonder.

Have I been so busy that I have missed the beauty of life? Have I been so occupied collecting information that I have missed the deep inner peace that should be mine? What am I going to do?

I will drop activities that I thought would fulfill me and didn't. I will let go of my need to know everything, and I will begin to listen to see if I am still here.

If more got me to where I am, I can only conclude that less will get me to where I want to be.

The System

I am a part of our system where we take from the poor and give to the rich.

What to do when I don't approve of the system and still must exist within it?

I will conduct my affairs in a manner that is acceptable to me, regardless of the cost.

I choose to accept that which I cannot change, support those who are trying, and to share whatever I have of value in a loving and nonpossessive way.

No matter how little or how much I have, I will always have some gift to share.

This is not great benevolence; it is the natural way.

I will therefore stay in the natural flow of the universe while living within the system.

Unfair

Life is unfair. . . . Why?

Who knows. Even the wisest of the wise and all of the scientific resources have not given us an answer to this.

In the universal order, it seems that regardless of the species, some are protected and some lead difficult and short lives.

The randomness in the universal order is unexplainable.

I will accept my place in the universe and embrace the mother of all things, and all of my needs will be provided.

There is a universal plan. I just don't understand it.

Life Overvalued

Life is cheap for the oppressed and distressed.

Risks are not really risks when one has nothing to lose.

When I have everything material and nothing of the spirit, life is without meaning and death seems a reasonable alternative.

Birth, life, and death are all a part of the same process. They are the process.

Knowing this, I live day by day with no thought of life or death.

So why did I overvalue life and fear death? I was afraid of losing that which I thought I had, even though I didn't have it.

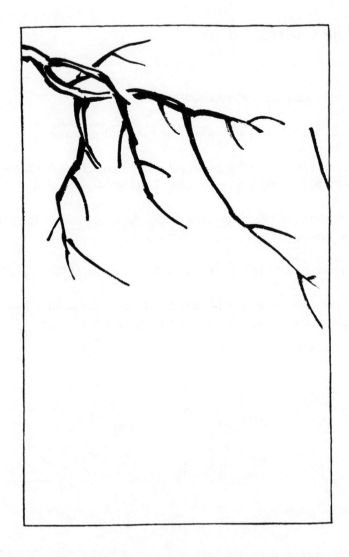

Withered and Dry

Green and supple are the characteristics of life; withered and dry denote death.

When I was middle-aged and miserable, I was withered and dry and for all intents and purposes dead. Recovery has changed all that.

Finding my place in the universal order has given me life as I have never known it: acceptance, adaptability, flexibility of both mind and body, and the peace that surpasses all peace.

Young or old, we all have the same choice, withered and dry or green and supple.

I choose to live and die as the young dogwood or the fresh twig of the maple.

Helping But Hurting

I want to make a difference in this world by helping others. I have tried in the past, and for some reason it has not worked. Something is missing.

People do not seem to want to give up their beliefs and adopt mine. Maybe I should consider allowing others to own those feelings and ideas that seem important to them.

After all, I do know that the truly significant and lasting principles come from the universal center and not from we mortals.

Am I not grounded enough in the universe to grant others, whom I intend to help, the privilege of finding their own way to serenity?

I will use restraint in dealing with others and open myself up to the infinite possibilities of the great unknown.

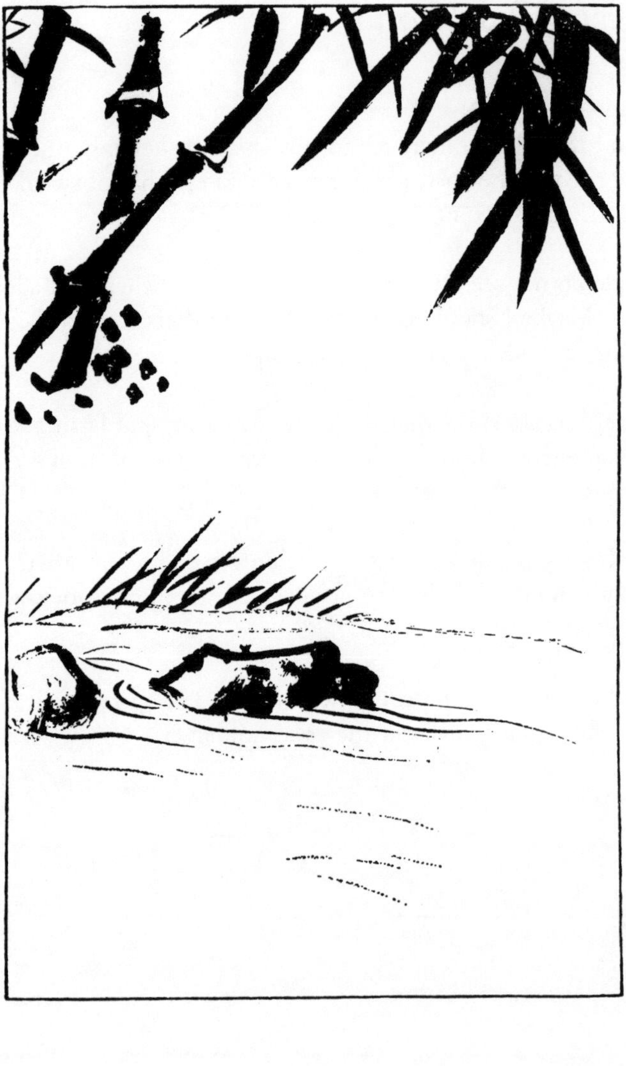

Work Without Working

Darkness that is nothing overcomes everything.

That without substance goes everywhere.

I think about the truly natural artists, musicians, and athletes and the apparent ease with which they perform: loose . . . relaxed . . . concentrated.

I think about the great who were not gifted but who got there with tremendous effort and sacrifice . . . admirable but very stressful.

So I can either fight my work, or I can relax and find my natural and joyful self who knows no other way to live than to let go.

Force

The use of force causes resistance.

Resistance causes the loss of strength.

The universe, our world, nations, and people all resist the use of force, ultimately sapping the strength of those who apply the force.

The result is turmoil and despair and war.

There are gentle and effective ways of achieving results that do not involve glory, boasting, and pride.

My place in the universal order allows me to accomplish that which is mine to do without the use of force.

What a wonderful realization!

Nonviolence

Detachment leaves no room for violence.

Violence is often caused by those who believe that their way is the only way. Zealots demand that everyone adopt their beliefs.

In the way of the spirit there is room for all beliefs. They are a part of the One.

The oppressed are tempted to violently overthrow the oppressor.

There is another way . . . nonviolent resistance.

Detachment and humility help one avoid violence and still enjoy the fruits of life.

I See Without Looking

I have traveled the world, I have seen everything and I have seen nothing.

The more I know, the less I know.

I have been seeing and listening in the wrong places. If this is not true, why are not my overprivileged friends and I content?

My beautiful Great Mother told me to look inward and find contentment.

Look at the trees, and see everything.

Listen to the birds and the wind blowing through the trees, and hear all the sounds.

Maybe it is time for me to listen in the right place and to my Great Mother who knows.

Could she be right?

PART IV

LIVING

Community

Recovery leads to a sense of community.

Recovering people have a common bond.

Recovering people treat each other as longtime friends.

Recovering people become simple and honest with themselves.

Recovering people have a sense of their mortality.

Recovering people consider their fellows as their family.

Recovering people allow their fellows to live and die with respect.

Recovering people are special . . . but they are ordinary.

Nature

In the spiritual world nothing is demanded, not even respect for spirit. Respect is in the natural order of things.

In true love, nothing is demanded. True love allows freedom and respect for the beloved.

Our lives are influenced by our environment, sometimes resulting in hardship and sometimes unbelievable unity. Nature can be viewed as an enemy to be conquered, or as spirit that ebbs and flows from birth to death.

Respect, honor, and virtue will be a part of me when I find my center and live in the spirit of infinite bliss. Respecting and protecting nature, being one with the air, the sky, and the land, no matter in what surroundings I find myself, is the way of universal order.

Obligations

My relationships with others have suffered because we have each failed to fulfill that which we perceived to be obligations to each other.

Do you really want me to perceive your obligations for you? I can assure you that I don't want you to perceive mine.

I now accept that I can't make you adopt my perceptions as yours, but I can let you know what they are, and I am open to your ideas about mine.

Hopefully, we will grow into a better understanding of each other and above all have a greater willingness to keep our own half of the bargain.

It is inevitable that we will sometimes fail. I will try to understand.

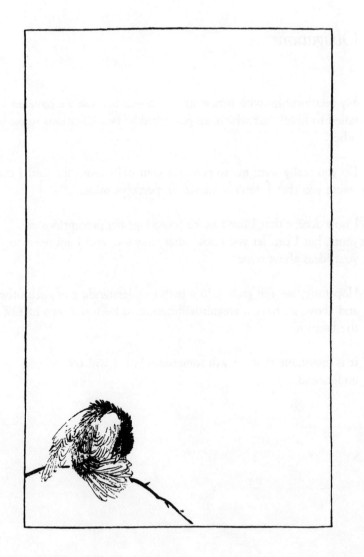

A Small Risk

It is exhausting to rush about doing work, caring for family, caring for others, and looking for answers in all the wrong places.

There must be a better way.

How much better to be constant and easy and spend time with myself. Then I have the energy and self-esteem to share myself with others.

If I don't have "it," I cannot give "it" to you.

At times I find myself doubting the validity of the quiet way. Maybe I will get to the point of desperation where I will be willing to try it.

Or hopefully, I will take the small risk of sitting down quietly and listening to my inner voice and see how I like it.

A small risk with potential rewards of giant proportions.

Detachment

I look around and see those who share their strength and wisdom with others and wonder what it is they have and that I admire. They seem to enjoy being out of the limelight and are so comfortable with themselves that I am always comfortable with them.

To be interested in me and yet not take on my burdens nor tell me what to do is respectful, and it is the kind of relationship that I can joyfully accept.

I accept that my best chance to have strength and wisdom is to grow quietly and remain detached in a healthy way from all things that might detract from my spiritual enlightenment.

Being in the background lessens the distractions.

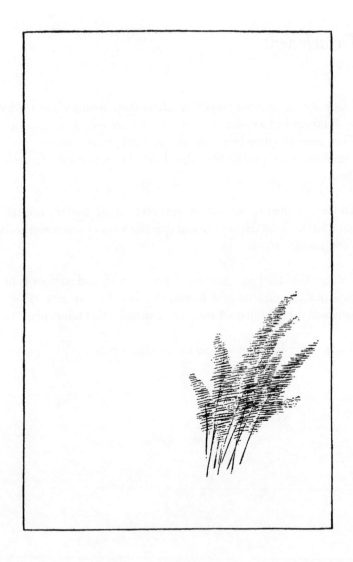

I Am Restless

I am not grounded, and I have no roots!

Everything is exaggerated. If it weren't, my life would be unbearably boring. I know that what I am looking for is out there and I would find it if I would just look harder.

However, I am aware of a few calm and peaceful people who, strangely enough, do not seem bored. When I think back, I remember that some of these serene people were just like I am, a few years ago.

I am tired of running and trying to find myself. I believe I will decide to allow myself to become one of those calm and peaceful people by going back to my roots in the natural order of things.

I am ready.

Moderation

I talk so much that I don't think you know what I am talking about.

You share sincerely and briefly, and I understand.

Tremendous gales are destructive and don't last long. Gentle, steady breezes nourish and replenish the earth forever.

I will become moderate in my talk and my actions and become one with the universe. Then you will be my friend and confidant.

That is my wish for myself.

Low Lands

Coastal low lands are female in nature. Open . . . receptive . . . quiet . . . tranquil.

My newfound recovering friends are like the low lands. All good seems to flow down to them and they have become aware and receptive.

Their spirits have become rich and fertile.

Their intuition has directed them.

Their roots are down.

They are tied to heaven like the marsh with its rains and mists.

I am grateful for my beautiful recovering friends.

Motives

I have done all of the right things to gain prestige and success. Donating and volunteering for the right causes has paid off. I am honored and respected.

So why do I envy my friend who quietly shares herself with all people and all causes, even those that might be called bad? She is not concerned with applause and recognition. What are her rewards?

Could it be that the deeds and money are not as important as the motives involved?

Giving with no expectation of reward is foreign to me. However, when I think of it, the way of the spirit is just that.

The supply is inexhaustible, is constantly available, and is gifted with no strings attached.

Heroes

I no longer consider our traditional heroes as role models.

Now there is the Great Mother.

In the past I considered heroes as God-like.

We are all the same.

We are all embraced by the Great Mother, who aimlessly and silently holds nothing back.

Nothing more can be said.

This is how it is!

Leaders Are Not Leaders

There are those who present themselves as ordinary folk but who have something about them that makes the rest of us want to follow them. These are truly leaders.

Their understanding of the true nature of things and their openness to the new lets us love and respect them without the fear that they will need to dominate or control.

Simple, open, and nonthreatening love is rare in our present culture.

Yes, deep down I know that these are the true leaders.

Chaos Attracts "Experts"

The world is full of sick people who get their self-worth from advising other sick people. I will be eternally grateful for those wise souls who loved themselves enough to love me enough to let me find my own way.

It is easy for me to grasp for any thread of hope when the chaos of dysfunctional living is a part of my life and it is tempting to ask for advice. No one else can solve my problems. They can only share their experiences, strength, and hope.

Letting go is the answer.

I will love those who offered advice, since they were doing the best they could.

I will revere those who let me get my answers from that place beyond, where there is order, balance, and harmony.

Cleverness

I don't trust clever people.

If things are not simple and straightforward, it seems that something is being withheld from me.

Cleverness seems to be the order of the day . . . quick deals, competitive relationships, instant success, and the smugness that goes with putting something over on someone. How sick!

My intention is to avoid the spectacular and complicated and to lead a quiet and serene life.

There is no room for ego trips, no matter what the circumstances.

When I am tempted to be one of the clever ones, I will remember, NO EGO TRIPS TODAY.

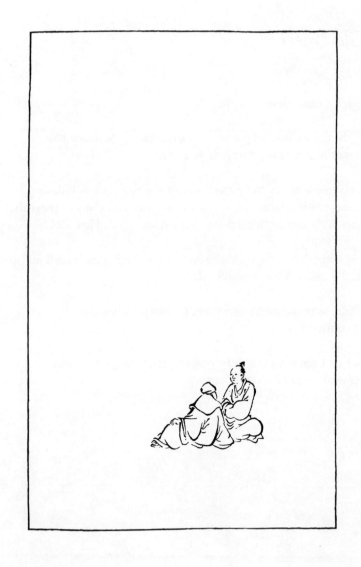

Cunning and Baffling

I have observed three stages of mind that seem to be typical of those of us in recovery.

Suddenly I realized that I had gone through them myself. It is hard now to believe that I had been so egoistic as to believe that I had all the answers.

GREAT WISDOM—"I will now tell you how you should proceed on your path."

GREAT KINDNESS—"I will help you with any of your problems."

GREAT INGENUITY—"We can make a fortune with this deal."

Does it sound familiar? It makes me squirm!

Now that I am aware of these excesses I am letting go of them and returning to the humble, simple life where I can realize my true nature.

Meddling

I used to meddle in others' affairs, and they didn't seem to appreciate my help.
I now allow others the dignity of running their own lives.

I used to strive for perfection, and my striving created tension and resentment in those around me.
I now accept my limitations and forgive my imperfections.

I used to be loud and boastful, and people avoided me.
I now live a quiet and peaceful life.

I used to demand more than my share, and people cheated me.
I now accept my share with gratitude.

I am now appreciated, helpful, and wanted and
I always get my share.

I am loved.

Minding My Own Business

"I have told you and I have told you . . ." I cringe when I think of the times when I said that to you.

The preposterous part is that I expected you to hear me. How could you in your alcoholic daze? Why would you when attacked like that?

Learning that I could only change myself relieved me of the awful feelings of responsibility for you and gave me a sense of freedom that was completely new to me.

Now that I have learned to "mind my own business," you are free to begin your recovery whenever and if ever you choose.

Nonaction Is Not No-action

Absorbing the idea of minding my own business and letting you take care of yours was difficult to say the least.

Absorbing the idea that the best way to mind my business was to take on the idea of nonaction until things settled down was even worse.

Amazingly, as the nonaction mode resulted in a realization of the potential spiritual gifts that could be mine, loving actions began to happen that required no decisions on my part.

Now the spirit of nonaction connects me to the universal order in such a way that actions flow constantly and lovingly.

I cannot explain nonaction, I can only experience it.

Where Are All the Others?

Recovery is easy when we understand the process.

Recovery is hard if we try to do it by ourselves.

Yielding to the universal order is the secret to recovery the easy way.

Losing oneself totally to the spiritual way is frightening. The rewards are awesome. Few have gone that far.

We have made that leap of faith to the unknown and the world of infinite bliss.

Where are all the others who have not yet joined us on the path to recovery?

We will wait for them with open arms.

Judge Not—Fear Not

If I am serious about my recovery, I will avoid those things that will impede my progress.

By loving you and all others enough to let you go, I have no need to judge anyone, including myself. This leaves me free to put the focus on me and allow my place in the universal order to manifest.

By not judging you, I have no need to fear you.

By not fearing you, I have no need to judge you.

By transposing "you" to "universe," I have nothing to fear, including death.

Virtue

I can dream about a virtuous universe, or I can put virtue to work, right where I am.

Fantasy versus reality.

Some of us are, by nature, activists, and some of us do not fit that role. Neither is good nor bad—just different.

I am not an activist, but by living my life with integrity, I will be doing that which is possible for me.

A beautiful me affects my family first, friends next, then my village, then my nation, and finally the universe.

Whether large or small, my contribution is important . . . and possible.

What Is Great

Great is two things. Great is sometimes so perfect that it is an illusion. The other great is often not obvious and is hard to recognize, but it is real.

I can be great without being perfect and without anybody knowing I am great.

I don't need to be a great orator to tell you that I love you and mean it.

I don't need to be the perfect husband to share my imperfections with you.

I don't need to be a genius to reason with you and understand you.

Honesty and simplicity are great.

Small and Simple Are Great

The flow of the universe is simple.

I will not become confused by the tumult that is all around me. It could be overwhelming and give me a clouded vision of the world.

The reality is to find greatness in doing those simple acts that are within my ability to perform naturally. In the universal order great acts are made up of small acts.

If I understand that difficulties require only small actions, I will respond without delay.

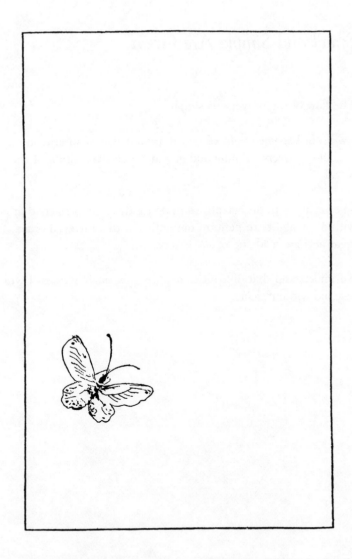

Living But Dead

There are those who live life and love it, those who hate life and flaunt death, and those who simply pass from birth to death without living.

Which one have I been? Which one am I to be now?

I am starting on the path of enlightenment, where I accept both life and death as the natural order of things.

My life will be free of the fear of death and dullness, violence and cowering, and will be filled with beauty, peace, and spontaneous joy.

The past is over, but the future is here and now. . . . I am ready.

Responsibility

Responsibility for the world is unbearable.

Responsibility for employees is demanding.

Responsibility for loved ones leads to feelings of guilt for past errors and failure to live up to expectations of oneself.

A truly compassionate leader is immersed in the spirit of the universe and has found security and protection for herself and others in the Great Mother.

I will love others enough to let them go. I trust that finding my center and the attendant peace will somehow result in protection and nurturing for all.

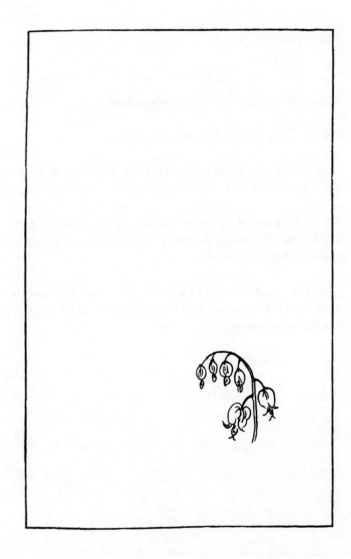

Abandonment

Recovery from abandonment is hard. . . . It is a matter of regaining trust.

In order never to experience the feeling of abandonment again, one must become secure within oneself. Then leaving will not be abandonment.

The spiritual way is the way of real security.

Trust your higher power.

Trust yourself.

Trust your family.

Trust your friends.

Finally trust that you are in exactly the right place at the right time.

There will be no abandonment.

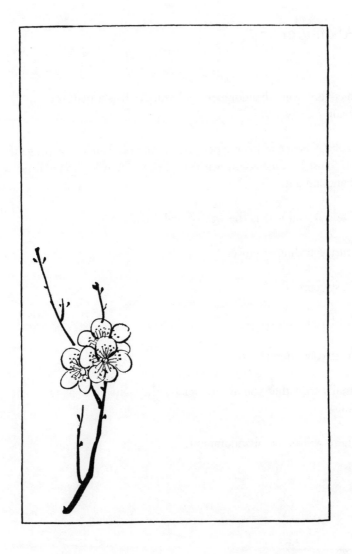

Hope

There have been times when I was simply not capable of dedication to anything, let alone something as demanding as the need for spiritual enlightenment.

I have changed. . . .

When there was no hope, I found hope.

When there were no friends, I found friends.

When there was no money, I found money.

When there was no help, I found help.

When there was no me, I found Me.

The grim and impossible always led me to perfect answers when I opened myself to the ever-present power of the universal order.

Abundance

Letting go a little improves life.

Letting go a lot brings happiness and joy.

Letting go of all things brings about an abundance of all things.

By letting go of all things, I become a child of the universe.

Being a child of the universe, I rest in the Great Mother. . . .

And all things flow down to me in unbelievable abundance.

I am fulfilled, and I am grateful.